D0516485

CLEANING UP OUR WATER

Linda Goldman

Technical Consultant
Sharon Saari, President
The Idea Center, Inc.

CHILDRENS PRESS®
CHICAGO

A production of B&B Publishing, Inc.

Editor – Jean Black
Photo Editor – Margie Benson
Computer Specialist – Katy O'Shea

Interior Design – Jean Black/Dave Conant
Artist: Barbara Hammer

Library of Congress Cataloging-in-Publication Data

Goldman, Linda 1946-
    Cleaning up our water / by Linda Goldman.
        p. cm.
    Includes index.
    ISBN 0-516-05543-7
    1. Water quality management -- United States -- Juvenile literature.
2. Water -- Pollution -- United States -- Juvenile literature. [1. Water quality
management. 2. Water -- Pollution] I. Title.
TD223.G65 1994
333.91'137--dc20   94-18025
                                                                 CIP
                                                                 AC

Cover photo: Children play in a lake in Los Padres National Forest in California.

Title Page: Father and son fish in the waters of Lake Tahoe, California.

Table of Contents Page: Two students learn how to test water quality at Head Arboretum in Madison, Wisconsin.

PHOTO SOURCES

Cover Photo: © Rob Badger
Air India 39; City of Arcata, California 63; Courtesy of the British Tourist Authority 40; Bureau of Reclamation, Lower Colorado Region 8 right; California Department of Water Resources 8 top, 79 bottom, 83; Canadian Park Service/J. Beardsell 73; Canadian Wildlife Service/Quebec Region 68; Clayton County, Georgia, Water Authority 89; © Chuck Davis Photo 79 left; Environmental Concern Inc. 60; © Kip Evans 57; Florida Department of Commerce, Division of Tourism 9, 58 left; FAO photo by J. Isaac 14 left; Friends of the Crooked River 6 top; Ford North America Operations 24; Photo by Robert B. Genualdi, courtesy of Arizona Geological Survey 82; Terry Gips 14 bottom; Photo by Bonnie Gruber 12; Heal the Bay 75 both; Carrol Henderson 15, 36; Illinois EPA 50; Industry, Science, and Technology Canada Photo 42; © Breck P. Kent; Kerr-McGee 70; Kinsa/Kodak Photo Contest 41; © Gary Kramer 56; Lake Pontchartrain Basin Foundation 51 both; Lake Waramaug Task Force/Thomas McGowan 49 both; Justine Magsig/Sugar Creek Protection Society 37, 38; Reprinted with permission of Milwaukee Metropolitan Sewage District 23 both; National Aeronautics and Space Administration 19, 55; NOAA/Hazardous Materials Response Branch 67; NOAA/Marin Debris Information Office/S. Santona 71; © Richard Nowitz 84; Ocean Arks International 64; Ohio EPA/Bob Wysenski 4, 5, 47, 48 top; Ohio Lake Erie Office 13, 48 left; © Robert Queen Photo 3, 6, 52, 54, 80; Sharon Saari/The Idea Center 44, 58 top; City of St. Petersburg, Florida 29; City of Santa Barbara, California 18; Francis Smith 35; Soil Science Society of America 11 left, 81; South Florida Water Management District 33 bottom, 34 both, 45 bottom, 59; Southern California Edison 78; Al Stenstrup 88; Surfrider Foundation 76, 77; Tennessee Valley Authority/Water Quality Department 61 top & middle, 90 top; Melissa Turner 17, 27, 28 both; U.S. Air Force Photo/McClellan Air Force Base 87; U.S. Army Corps of Engineers/St. Louis District 30, 31, 33 top; U.S. Army Corps of Engineers/New Orleans District 11 right, 32; U.S. Coast Guard 66, 69 right; U.S. EPA/S.C. Delaney 10; U.S. Fish and Wildlife Service 61 bottom, 65; Gavin Villareal 69 bottom; Weidinger Public Relations 1, 45 top; J. Conrad Williams © 1988 Newsday 86; Terri Willis 91; Wisconsin Department of Natural Resources 22, 46, 53, 74, 85; World Bank Photo Library 20 top, 90 left

CONTENTS

Water—Our Most Precious Resource

Today the restored Cuyahoga River in Ohio (above) is clean enough for pleasure boating.

Every year the people of Ohio hold a "River-Day." People spend the morning of RiverDay removing trash from the river and its banks. Then, they take part in programs that teach them how to keep the river healthy. Concerts, games, canoe floats, and picnics round out the day.

The people are celebrating the rebirth of the Cuyahoga River, which runs through Cleveland and Akron. The Cuyahoga is clean again. But it once was so filled with garbage and other waste that it caught fire!

Imagine a river burning with flames shooting almost five stories high. The Cuyahoga was shouting for help. A river where people once fished on long summer days had become a bad-smelling, dirty waterway. Fish that could live in its waters were too deadly for anyone to eat.

People dumped garbage and chemicals into the Cuyahoga River for many years. By 1936, it had so much rotten trash in it that it bubbled stinking gas. Some parts of the river carried more bacteria and germs than are found in sewers. Then the accumulation of waste, oil, and gas started to burn. Fires broke out on the river from time to time over the next 33 years! One fire lasted two days!

By 1969, the people of Cleveland and Akron were demanding that the government do something to help. Laws were passed forbidding the dumping of raw, or untreated, waste into the river. New wastewater-treatment plants were built to clean up city and industrial water before it entered

bacteria = one-celled living things that may cause disease; so small that they can be seen only with a microscope.

The worst fire on the Cuyahoga River occurred in 1952. The waste and oil on the river burned for two days.

pollution = harmful chemicals or other materials that don't belong in the environment.

the river. The Cuyahoga was gradually able to clean itself. Finally, fish could swim in it, and animals and birds could safely drink its waters again.

It cost industry and government millions of dollars to clean up this river. It is once again a lovely place where Ohioans can enjoy the day.

A group called Friends of the Crooked River has become the Cuyahoga's watchdog. They help identify and fix the river's problems today. The Friends and other area residents are determined to keep their river a good place to go fishing and boating—or just to enjoy the outdoors. RiverDay reminds people that while they were successful in cleaning up their river, they have to work to keep it that way.

Sadly, the Cuyahoga River is not the only body of water in the world to suffer from pollution. Many of our rivers, lakes, oceans, and underground water sources have severe pollution problems. And when our waterways are in trouble, we are in trouble, too.

Many people enjoy fishing. But if the water is polluted, the fish are not safe to eat.

Today we need water for drinking and many industrial uses. We also enjoy water for all kinds of recreation.

Making Use of the Water

All living things need water. Of course, fish, shellfish, seaweed, dolphins, and whales live in it. But land animals and plants require water, too. We need it to drink and bathe in. We can't survive without it.

Since prehistoric times, human beings have depended on oceans, rivers, and lakes for transportation as well as for food and water. We also use rivers and waterfalls to make electrical power for our cities, homes, and factories.

For centuries, people used freshwater lakes and rivers to take baths, wash clothes, and carry body wastes away from living areas. As the waters tossed and turned, the waste products broke up into smaller and smaller parts. Eventually they became part of the soil or food for sea life.

Rivers are dammed to provide electric power. This is the Hoover Dam on the Colorado River.

Only about 3 percent of the Earth's water is fresh water. About 75 percent of this fresh water is frozen in glaciers and ice caps of the Arctic and Antarctic. Much of the remaining fresh water is stored underground. The rest of the fresh water fills rivers, lakes, swamps, and marshes.

In early times, most products humans used were made of materials supplied by nature. So they were biodegradable—they could be broken down by nature. Nature could deal with everything we tossed aside—paper, straw, wood, cloth, bones, dye, and even leather. We thought our oceans, rivers, and lakes would stay healthy no matter what we threw into them. But we were wrong. In many ways we hurt them badly.

The Industrial Age

Over the centuries, the human population of the world has multiplied. The amount of waste we dispose of has increased also.

During the 1700s, the Industrial Revolution began. People started to use machines in their work, recreation, and households. More recently, skillful scientists and engineers developed many new kinds of materials that were made in laboratories. Nature didn't make these materials—and nature could not dispose of them either.

Our garbage dumps, junkyards, and wastebaskets overflow with materials that are not biodegradable. Many of the things we throw away—fast-food containers, Styrofoam cups, bat-

As the population grows, cities such as Miami, Florida, get larger and need more clean water.

9

teries, polyester clothing, car parts, rubber tires, television sets, broken phones—will be around long after we are dead.

The rise of industry also meant that more water was used. Many factories use water to keep machines from getting too hot. Every day, they pump hundreds of thousands of gallons of water through their plants.

As the water cools the hot machines, it picks up many chemicals and oils. Sometimes these poisonous materials are dumped into our rivers and lakes along with the used water. When this dumping goes on year after year, the water gradually becomes polluted. We cannot drink it, and fish cannot live in it.

Make Room for People

Some of the world's richest farmland lies along riverbanks. When a river overflows its banks and floods onto the land, it carries tons of soil with it. This soil is rich in nutrients that help plants grow, so farmers use it for growing crops.

nutrients = substances needed by plants and animals to grow and live.

But many people didn't want to let rivers flood. They wanted to build farms and towns along the rivers, but such places could be damaged by floods. In order to prevent floods from going into farms and cities, people built walls, dams, and canals to control rivers. People also have drained many swamps and marshes. These former wetlands are then used by farmers and builders.

So we kept making changes to our waterways. And for many years we ignored the damage we were doing. Each change people make to the natural environment affects all the plants and animals that live there. Perhaps a small plant or insect can no longer survive because the soil has become too dry. Fish that swam in a wetland have nowhere to go when the water is gone.

wetland = land that has water standing in it all or part of the year.

The wetlands of the Red River in Louisiana are now used for farming and pastureland (left). Along the Mississippi River, people have built walls called levees to hold the water back. Levees destroyed the natural wetlands (above).

All life fits together like a jigsaw puzzle. When one species of plant or animal dies out because of a change in its environment, other plants and animals suffer also. Water is one of the most important parts of the environment. And people easily can change the amount and quality of this most precious resource.

Animals depend on water to live just as people do.

Agricultural Pollution

To feed the growing millions of people on this planet, farmers turned to science for help. They found that plants produced more vegetables and fruits with artificial fertilizers than with natural fertilizers such as manure from farm animals.

To keep insects from eating crops, farmers also

started to use poisons called pesticides. But many of these pesticides poison other animals, too.

These chemicals poison everything they touch. When it rains, the water picks up the fertilizers and pesticides. The polluted water then runs off into rivers and lakes. The water also may soak into the ground, carrying those dangerous chemicals with it. Then the water that lies underground may be poisoned.

pesticides = chemicals that kill insects, weeds, and other pests on crops.

Finding Solutions

It is increasingly clear that Earth's oceans, rivers, lakes, and wetlands can't handle the wastes and poisons we throw in them. Our beaches are littered with trash and untreated human and animal wastes. Many lakes already have died—all plant and animal life poisoned. When birds eat fish containing certain pesticides, they lay eggs with shells too thin to survive.

Today many people who live near waterways work to clean up beaches. These people are picking up trash on a beach in Ohio.

The people who study water sources are working hard to find solutions. Some of their ideas are discussed in this book.

Tons of industrial, city, and agricultural wastes still find their way into our water every year. So our first job is to stop polluting our waterways. But prevention is only part of the answer. Many waterways need help to restore the purity of their water.

We also must find better ways to use the clean water we have, to stop wasting water, and to find new sources of clean, safe water. In North America and Europe, we take a drink of clean fresh water for granted—we just turn on the faucet. We know the water will be clear and free of dirt or waste. But how long will this last? You probably will have enough clean water as long as you live. But what about your children?

The answers aren't easy. Water needs increase daily. Do we stop building new factories? Do we stop progress? Could we live as simply as people lived a thousand years ago? Probably not. Instead, we must find ways to balance our growing needs with our planet's water resources.

In developing countries such as India (above) and Burkina Faso (right), water is not as clean or as plentiful as in North America. But people still have to use it for drinking and for growing crops.

Fresh water can be found in remote areas such as the Falls of the Rio Quijos in Ecuador, South America. However, getting it where it is needed can be a problem.

A Cup Here, a Gallon There

After you got up this morning, you probably went to the bathroom, washed your hands, brushed your teeth, and then sat down for breakfast. Let's say you had a glass of milk, half a grapefruit, and a slice of toast with margarine.

How much water do you think you used? Three gallons? Four gallons? Look at the chart to find out.

By the time breakfast is finished, the average person uses about 233 gallons (882 liters) of water. In two days, the children in an average-size school classroom use enough water to fill a swimming pool—just in freshening up and eating breakfast.

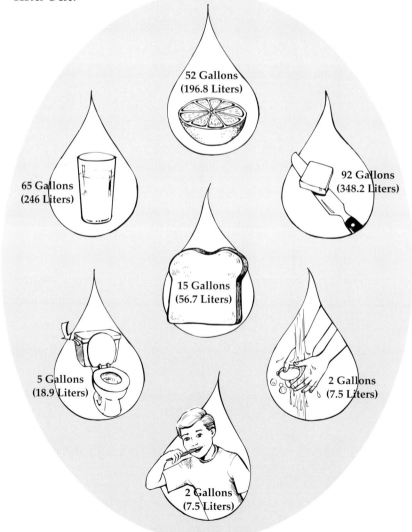

52 Gallons (196.8 Liters)

65 Gallons (246 Liters)

92 Gallons (348.2 Liters)

15 Gallons (56.7 Liters)

5 Gallons (18.9 Liters)

2 Gallons (7.5 Liters)

2 Gallons (7.5 Liters)

"Wait a minute!" you might argue. "I didn't drink 65 gallons (246 liters) of milk. I drank only one glass. How could that chart be right?"

But think about it. In order to produce milk, cows must be watered. Their feed must be grown. Their dairy must be washed down. The amount of water used to take care of their needs was figured into your glass of milk.

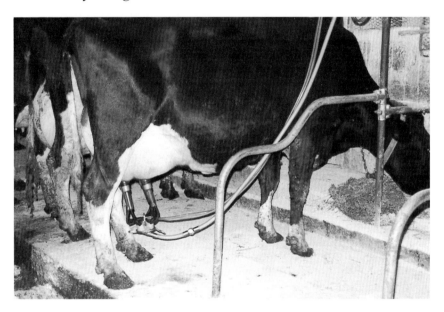

A dairy farm uses large amounts of water to produce the milk we drink every day.

Actually, an average family of four uses 2,500 to 4,500 gallons (9,460 to 17,028 liters) of water every week. That includes the water used to drink, cook, shower, wash the car, do laundry, and flush the toilet.

Water, Water Everywhere

Why is it important for us to be aware of the ways we use water? Why do people keep telling us

The People Beat a Three-Year Drought!

From 1988 to 1990, southern California faced a serious drought. Year after year of very little rain had caused a severe water shortage. The people of Santa Barbara, California, had to find other water sources—or make some major changes.

Everyone worked at saving water. People took shorter showers.

They turned off the water while soaping up and stepped into cold water instead of waiting for the hot water. They didn't flush toilets every time they used them. Water used for cooking and washing hands was saved and used to water plants. Many people gave up their lawns and flower beds to save water.

People checked their plumbing for more ways to save water. They installed water-saving nozzles in their showers and special toilets that flushed with less water. They promptly fixed all leaky pipes and dripping faucets. Restaurants didn't serve water unless a customer asked for it.

The price of water was raised. People were fined if they used more water than they were allowed. Three police officers traveled around the city giving tickets to people who wasted water by washing cars or watering lawns.

The city of Santa Barbara cut water usage by over 30 percent! And the water-saving habits the people learned during the drought still are practiced today, after the drought has ended.

to "save" water? After all, more than 70 percent of the Earth is covered with water. Isn't that more water than we could ever use?

We can't use ocean water directly to solve our water problems. Humans can't drink salt water. It would make us very sick. Farmers can't use it because it would ruin their crops.

Remember, only 3 percent of all the water on this planet is fresh water. And that is all the water there will ever be. Just as important as cleaning up our water sources is being careful not to use more water than we need.

The Life of a Raindrop

It's impossible to see where a circle begins. You can start anywhere and follow the circle around without missing anything. The Earth's water cycle is like a circle.

All of the water on our planet has been here for millions of years. Dinosaurs sipped the same water you drink today. Every drop of Earth's water has traveled through the water cycle many times. When the sun shines on a water surface, it warms the water, causing it to evaporate, or change into water vapor. This invisible vapor rises into the atmosphere, where it may form clouds.

evaporate = change from a liquid into a gas.

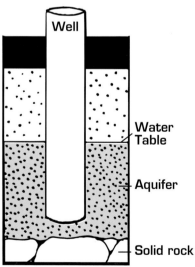

Well

Water Table

Aquifer

Solid rock

Each time it rains or snows, some of the vapor in the atmosphere becomes liquid again and falls back to the Earth's surface. There, it can follow many paths. Some liquid finds its way into rivers, lakes, and oceans. Other raindrops are taken up by plants or trees. The water then evaporates back into the air again from the leaves. Animals also drink the water caught by leaves.

Most rain falls onto the ground, where it seeps into the soil. The water flows down through little cracks and holes between the rocks and soil grains. Eventually it reaches the large underground rock formations called aquifers. The top of the water in an aquifer is called the water table. The water table rises and falls depending on the amount of rainfall.

Water moves through the rocky aquifer like it would rise through a sponge. What happens when you put part of a sponge in water? The tiny pores, or holes, in the sponge allow the water to rise through it until the whole thing is wet.

Sometimes an aquifer holds so much water that it seems like an underground river or lake. In other places, it looks like wet sand on the beach.

Water in an aquifer moves very slowly. In some aquifers, the water travels several feet in a day. In others, it moves only a

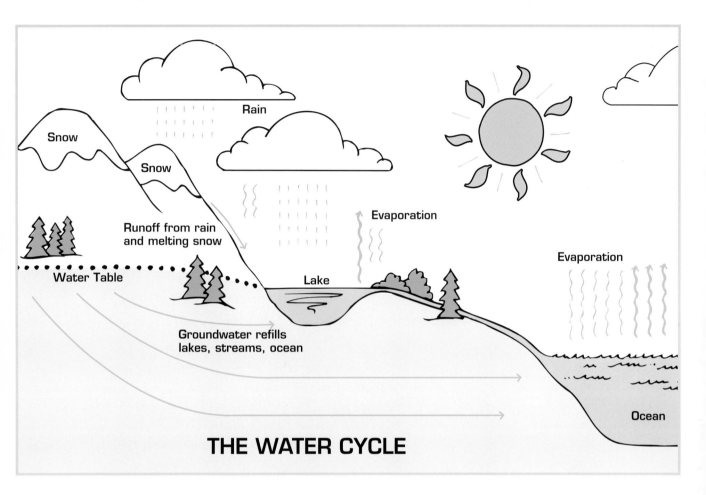

Snow

Snow

Rain

Evaporation

Evaporation

Runoff from rain
and melting snow

Water Table

Lake

Groundwater refills
lakes, streams, ocean

Ocean

THE WATER CYCLE

fraction of an inch in an entire year! But all aquifers have a rocky bottom that the water can't pass through.

People who live in the country often dig wells into aquifers for their water. Pumps bring the underground water up to the surface.

Rain and snow do not always end up as groundwater, however. Sometimes the ground may already be full of water—or covered with concrete. Then water that doesn't evaporate in the

groundwater = fresh water that moves through and among the rocks underground.

runoff = water that runs over the surface of the ground before reaching a lake, a river, or the ocean.

Humans treat water to make it safe to drink.

parasite = any living thing that grows, feeds, and is sheltered at the expense of another.

sunshine runs directly into rivers or lakes. This water is called runoff. Runoff may first run into drains built under streets. But the water in drains eventually goes into rivers and lakes, too.

The water cycle isn't always so direct. Like other plants and animals, we humans drink water. Our cells need water as long as we are alive. We also manufacture products that contain water. That water may not return to the water cycle for hundreds of years.

But whatever path the raindrop takes, it eventually returns to the Earth's surface and evaporates into the atmosphere again.

Dropping Out of the Water Cycle

All living things take water out of the water cycle. Only humans, however, do things to change the water. First we treat it in a water-treatment plant to make it safe to drink or use in some other way. Finally, we usually clean the water in a wastewater-treatment, or sewage, plant before returning it to nature.

People have known for many years that it isn't safe to drink water directly from a water source. It might contain bacteria or parasites that cause disease. Or it might contain dangerous chemicals from a manufacturing plant or from farm fields. So our water is treated with various processes to make it safe to drink.

Many years ago people dumped the leftover

This plant in Wisconsin treats wastewater to make it safe before returning it to Lake Michigan.

water from washing clothes or cooking on the ground or into rivers or lakes. Today, with more than five billion people on Earth, the rivers, lakes, and oceans can't break down all the waste we add to water. We help by putting used water through a wastewater-treatment process.

Buildings in cities and towns have pipes that run underground. The pipes collect wastewater and carry it to a wastewater-treatment plant. There the water is cleaned before it is returned to the water cycle.

At the end of the wastewater-treatment process, two things emerge—cleaned water and sludge. The water is returned to the water cycle by pouring it into a river or lake. Sludge often gets further treatment so that it can be used to help our environment.

Cities in the United States today often use dried sludge in parks and golf courses as a natural fertilizer. Often, grass clippings

wastewater = water that has been used in some way and is no longer clean.

sludge = the almost solid material that settles out when used water is cleaned in a waste-water-treatment plant. Some people use dried sludge, such as Milorganite, (left) as fertilizer.

23

and tree trimmings are mixed with the sludge. This not only saves space in landfills but also adds nutrients to the sludge.

Enough Water for All?

Clearly, our planet's water is always moving through the water cycle and we never lose any water forever. So why isn't there enough water today?

The people of the world use water faster than nature can move it through the water cycle. Every day we North Americans use millions of gallons in our homes alone.

Factories use a great deal of water to cool machines. And water is used to wash down factory floors and the products manufactured there.

Sometimes water is used when a product is being made. Did you know it takes 39,090 gallons (147,920 liters) of water to make a new car? Or that making one pound (0.4 kilogram) of plastic uses 24 gallons (91 liters) of water?

And then there's the water used in big supermarket refrigerators to keep ice cream cold, and the water used to keep parks, golf courses, and lawns green. In power plants, water is boiled to produce steam for

Producing one car uses thousands of gallons of water.

Citywide Effort to Save Water

The 350,000 people of the area around Waterloo in Ontario, Canada, depend on groundwater to take care of their needs. During the 1970s, experts advised city leaders to look for other sources of water if they couldn't cut back on water usage.

Volunteers handed out kits to over 50,000 homes containing special plumbing equipment, such as toilet dams (right), that helped control the amount of water used. They also taught students how to conserve water at home. Laws were passed to force everyone to use less water. For instance, by 1996, all new toilets must use only 1.6 gallons (6 liters) of water with each flush. Older toilets use up to 5 gallons (19 liters) per flush.

In just three years, the people of Waterloo cut water use by 10 percent! And 20 years from now, they hope to be using only the same amount of water. It won't be easy, especially with new people and businesses moving into the city, but the people of Waterloo think the effort is worth it!

making electricity. Firefighters use water. So do restaurants and laundromats.

Wastewater-treatment plants return hundreds of millions of gallons of treated water to our lakes, rivers, aquifers, and oceans every day. But that's only half the amount we're taking out.

So, while we have the same amount of water

today as a million years ago, there's a lot less of it available at any given moment.

Using Less

What's the solution? We all have to stop using so much fresh water. You've read about the people in Santa Barbara, California. You may not be able to change things in your city by yourself, but perhaps you can start a water conservation (water saving) program in your school or your home. A faucet that leaks just one drop every second uses an additional four gallons (15 liters) of water a day! In a year, that adds up to over 1,400 gallons (5,298 liters)! If you have a dripping faucet, get your family to fix it.

You also can save water by wetting your toothbrush and then turning off the water while you brush your teeth. Instead of a long shower, take a five-minute one. And turn off the water while you soap up. As a resource, water is as valuable as gold or oil. It's time we started treating it that way.

Using Reclaimed Water

reclaimed water = wastewater that is partially cleaned and treated. It is used to water crops and lawns, but not to drink.

One of the best ways to save water is to reuse it. Some cities are finding different ways to reclaim, or reuse, water.

Two 20-story office buildings located at Jamboree Center in Irvine, California, have two sets of pipes carrying water into them. Most buildings have only one set of pipes bringing in fresh water for washing hands and drinking. But these buildings have a second set that brings water from a wastewater-treatment plant. The water meets all the health department requirements for drinking water, but it has a slight greenish tint. It is used to flush toilets and to water lawns and landscaped areas.

These buildings use 80 percent less fresh water than other buildings! Just think how much water we could save if all buildings were this water thrifty.

Water used for cooking can be saved and reused to water plants.

Reusing Water at Home

Even if your city doesn't reclaim wastewater, you can reuse water at home. The people of Santa Barbara were able to save so much water because they used "gray water." Gray water is water that comes from showers, bathtubs, and washing machines. Water that has not touched garbage, toilets, soiled diapers, or household cleaners generally can be safely used.

Gray water can be used to water lawns, trees, and flowers, and to wash cars and sidewalks. You probably can save enough water in one day to water all the plants around your house for a week!

Look around and see where water is wasted at your house. Do you run the water in your shower or sink for a minute, waiting for hot water? Catch that water in a bucket instead of letting it run down the drain.

Water can be saved and reused in many ways. Water from cooking can be used on plants (above). Many restaurants serve water only if you ask for it (right).

The City of Tomorrow

The people in St. Petersburg, Florida, have taken a step into the future. The entire city uses a system like the office building in Irvine. Instead of dumping their treated wastewater into nearby lakes or rivers, they've found ways to reuse every drop possible!

In the mid-1970s, St. Petersburg began using reclaimed water on lawns, parks, and golf courses. By 1992, about 30 percent of the water used by the city was reclaimed—more than 23 million gallons (87 million liters) of reclaimed water every day! Businesses that don't need drinking-quality water use reclaimed water. The city uses all the reclaimed water their wastewater-treatment plants can produce. Not one drop is dumped into rivers, lakes, or the ocean!

In 1992, St. Petersburg was the only U.S. city to have this kind of program. By the year 2000, the city hopes to provide reclaimed water to over 17,000 customers and to irrigate almost 9,000 acres (3,640 hectares) of land.

S
U
C
C
E
S
S

S
T
O
R
Y

Rivers: Water on the Move

In 1993, thousands of home and business owners fought the rivers of the Midwest as the water overflowed the banks. People added thousands of sand-filled bags to the tops of levees. These walls had been built to keep the river from overflowing. But they were failing.

On the worst day of the floods, the Mississippi River at St. Louis, Missouri, was almost 50 feet (15 meters) high. That's more than 38 feet (12 meters)—the size of a four-story building—deeper than normal for that time of year. Every 66 seconds enough water to fill a football stadium flowed past a measuring point in St. Louis!

Volunteers filled sandbags to hold back the rising river water.

Months later, people still were shoveling the mud, garbage, and water out of their houses. Some people just moved away, abandoning their homes, which were too filthy to live in.

Where did all this water come from? So much rain and snow fell in the Midwest throughout the year that the ground wasn't able to soak it all up. The extra water and melted snow ran into every creek, stream, or small

MISSISSIPPI RIVER ATTACKS ST. GENEVIEVE

St. Louis, Missouri, July 1993 — For the past month the people of St. Genevieve have been filling cloth bags with sand. Hour after hour they pile bags on top of the river walls in a desperate attempt to save their homes and businesses. It's taken volunteers three weeks to raise the wall to 43 feet (13 meters).

The weather service has predicted more rain. The U.S. Geological Survey warns the river might rise another five feet (1.5 meters) by the weekend. That means two feet (0.6 meter) of water will flood over the top of the wall. The residents are rushing into town to build the river wall even higher.

Already homes near the river have lakes in their backyards deep enough to row across. Their basements are full of the same water and filth that was floating in the river. Branches, chemicals from flooded farmlands, soil, and human and animal waste that were floating in the Mississippi River now cover sofas and beds.

According to officials, this is the worst flood of the last hundred years. They say it might be two to four months before the river water leaves the flooded areas. For the people of St. Genevieve, it might be the middle of winter before they can get back into their houses and start repairing all the damage. Rotted floors, broken walls, stinking carpets, and destroyed furniture may be all that's left.

river it could reach. Those small waterways, called tributaries, dumped the water into the Missouri and Mississippi rivers. Finally, all that water had nowhere to go but over the riverbanks.

Controlling the River

When the weather is hot and dry for a long time, a river's water can get quite shallow. But during the years when rainfall and snowfall are heavy, river water can rise so much that it floods nearby land. The land that sometimes floods is called the river's floodplain. Floodplains make rich farming land. Towns often are built on floodplains because transportation is easy on a river. But sometimes those towns have problems because the river still floods.

Levees do a good job of holding back river water during most flood periods. But they also can change the way a river flows. Levees may make a river straighter than it was naturally. Boats can sail more easily on straight rivers than on rivers that twist and turn.

This levee on the Mississippi River was built to protect people from floods.

Levees have cut more than 200 miles (320 kilometers) off the length of the Mississippi River between Cairo, Illinois, and New Orleans, Louisiana. Shipping on the Mississippi is very important to the United States. When a river is left alone, its natural curves and wide banks slow the flow of water. During flood times, its slower flow keeps the water from rising too quickly in one

During the 1993 flood, some levees were blown up to release some of the river water before it flooded cities and towns. Other levees broke on their own (left).

area. The water has time to spread out over a much larger area.

We really don't know enough about preventing serious floods. And many people think we should not try to prevent them at all. Instead, we should not build on floodplains.

The Kissimmee Question

The Kissimmee River in Florida is an example of damage no one expected. The Kissimmee had been shortened by adding a system of canals between the river bends, where there was marshy ground. The length of the 98-mile (158-kilometer) river was cut almost in half. This increased the amount of land available for farming and building.

Almost immediately, however, the people in the area saw that the animal and plant life of the river was dying. Soon, the damage caused by changing the river began to show even farther away—in

The Kissimmee River was a winding river before canals were built to straighten its flow.

Canals such as this one were built on the Kissimmee River to make traveling on the river more convenient for people.

In April 1994, a test ditch was filled to see what would happen if the Kissimmee River were returned to its original path.

Lake Okeechobee and the huge wetland area called the Everglades. Much of the Everglades region is included within the boundaries of Everglades National Park.

In 1970, biologists recommended that the Kissimmee's marshes be restored. The state of Florida reopened 13 miles (21 kilometers) of old river channel and nearby marshlands in 1986 and allowed the river to flow through them again. The South Florida Water Management District is working to rebuild marshes in order to restore and repair this important wetland area. Officials hope this will encourage the insects, plants—and eventually fish and other animals—to return. However, some experts fear it may be too late to repair the damage done.

No one intends to hurt a river. And all our money, energy, and time may not be enough to fix one. But everyone agrees it's worth trying.

People Make a Difference

The Quashnet River in Cape Cod, Massachusetts, was once known for its fine trout fishing. Then, in the late 1800s, farmers dammed up the river and turned the flooded land into cranberry bogs. But when farmers found better areas to grow cranberries, they moved away. Without the farmers to cut back plant growth in the river and the cranberry bogs, the river basin became a wide, brush-choked stream, almost like a dry jungle.

In 1976, area volunteers and an organization called Trout Unlimited began to restore the Quashnet River. They cut down the brush and planted trees along the riverbanks. Since strong pesticides used by the farmers had killed many helpful insects, the volunteers collected insects, crayfish, and amphibians from rivers and set them loose in the Quashnet.

Today, fresh river water flows through from upstream. Fish and plants now thrive in the river area. Within ten years, the Quashnet was restored from a clogged, useless stream to a healthy river.

Rivers and streams churn and roll over rocks. The water is naturally cleaned as impurities are broken down.

The Nature of Rivers

Left in their natural state, rivers have great powers to clean themselves. Rivers usually flow from other water sources, such as lakes or creeks formed from rain and snow runoff. New water is always available to keep the river moving. And flowing water usually can carry away anything that falls into it.

As river water rolls and churns on its journey downstream, leaves, branches, and other debris collide with rocks and underwater logs and branches. They gradually break down into smaller and smaller pieces. Eventually, the tiny particles are carried to the mouth of the river where they settle on the bottom. Anything that settles to the bottom of water is called sediment.

Sediment also settles on a river's floodplain. The land becomes rich in nutrients and is good for growing crops. Nutrients in and around a river

sediment = the matter, such as bits of leaves, dead animals, loose soil, and clay, that settles out of water and onto the bottom of a waterway.

also feed a large variety of plant and insect life. These, in turn, support fish. Animals come to drink the water the river provides.

Breaking a River's Cycle

Life in a river is a cycle, somewhat like the water cycle. Living things thrive near and in a river. When they die, they fall into the river and eventually become part of the sediment that nourishes new life. If one part of this cycle is broken, the rest of it suffers.

Accidents of nature can sometimes break this cycle. In northwest Ohio, major flooding caused trees to fall into some streams and rivers. Over the next several years, dirt and trash accumulated against the fallen trees. Finally, the water flow was almost blocked.

When farmers along Sugar Creek asked the government to build a channel so that water could flow around the log jams in their river, some people objected. They wanted to see if the river could fix itself instead of having people dig a new, artificial channel. The government gave them a year to come up with a solution.

The water flow of Sugar Creek in Ohio was almost stopped by debris.

Many volunteers removed all the trash and sediment from around the fallen trees. Then they cut

Today, Sugar Creek flows freely. Volunteers clean the channel each year.

apart and removed the big logs. When they were through, they had a real river with all its natural beauty and life.

For years, people thought that the rivers of the world could process, or break down, anything we dumped into them—just as it does with leaves and twigs. We believed the river would take care of it all eventually. But we were wrong!

Today, many of our rivers are dying. Plant life and fish can no longer survive in their waters.

The Ganges Story

The Ganges is India's most important river. To the Hindu people, this river is sacred and holy. For centuries, they have come to bathe in the Ganges, believing its waters will wash away their sins.

Until recently, many Indian cities along the Ganges dumped untreated waste back into the river. Raw waste, industrial chemicals, and wastewater from manufacturing plants and farmland found its way into the Ganges.

Eventually, more than 370 miles (597 kilometers) of the river became so polluted that nothing could live in it. The water was so dangerous to the health of people who bathed in it that the government finally decided to take action.

India's government and people have begun to make changes step by step. Today, they control the dumping of wastewater from factories. And farmers are learning to use chemicals properly so that fewer poisons get into the water from runoff.

Indians hope that the steps they are taking to save their river also will save the river dolphin, a very rare species. Only five types of river dolphins exist in the world today. All of them are in danger because of river pollution.

Fortunately, in cleaning up the Ganges, the Indian people have a good example to follow. The Thames River, the most important waterway in England, already has been cleaned up. Nature and determined people, working together, did the job.

The Hindu people of India believe the waters of the Ganges River are sacred. Bathing in its waters is a special religious practice.

No More Dumping

The Thames River runs through the city of London as it travels through the southern part of Great Britain to the North Sea. Londoners used to spend many happy Sundays biking along its shores. Then, in the 1950s, long stretches of the Thames River turned black and smelly. Years of dumping wastes into the water by industries and towns were killing the river. By 1963, fish could no longer survive in its waters.

The British government and its people were determined to save the river. Laws were passed requiring oil companies and boat owners to clean up spilled oil and gasoline. The towns along the river updated their sewage-treatment plants so that wastewater flowing into the Thames couldn't hurt the river water. But that was only the first step.

Nature took over. When the dumping stopped, the moving water churned the rocks and dirt on the bottom. Waste and other pollutants were separated from the sediment and pushed downstream to the ocean by the river's moving water.

As the poisons washed out and the water slowly became cleaner, plant and animal life returned to the river. Seeds took root along the shores.

The Thames River is much healthier now, with more than 100 kinds of fish in it. But it took more than 30 years for the river to restore itself after people learned to leave it alone.

On the Road to Good Health

A river uses moving water to restore itself. Every day, tributaries deliver clean water to the main river. Given a chance, most rivers can renew themselves with this fresh water. But we can't keep making it harder and harder for rivers to clean themselves. By reducing and removing the harmful effects of human civilization on nature, we can help the environment to recover. Because this process can take many years, nature needs our help now.

Canadians are working hard to clean up the water of the St. Lawrence River. Balancing the needs of industry and recreation such as fishing isn't an easy job.

Lakes Big and Small

Lake Superior (above) is the largest and the cleanest of the five Great Lakes.

Sometimes, as rivers flow, the water spreads out to form a larger body of water—a lake. And in some places, the ground dips into a low area that reaches all the way down to an aquifer. It fills with water, also forming a lake.

Lakes can be small enough to be called ponds or large enough to be one of the Great Lakes. The Great Lakes of North America hold 18 percent of the Earth's fresh surface water. They provide drinking water for more than 25 million people. Lakes act like huge storage basins for water. Cities draw fresh water from them, and many people come to lakes for recreation.

A lake is also full of life. Ducks, fish, and drag-onflies call it home. At dusk, deer, raccoons, and even a bobcat might enjoy a drink at the water's edge. A lake supports an entire community of both water-living and land-living plants and animals. The two groups depend on each other.

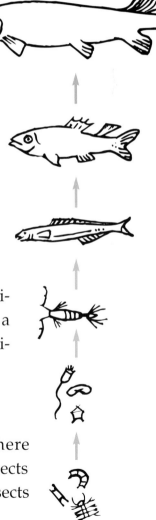

Tiny algae and single-cell animals are the bottom of the food chain, while small fish and insects are in the middle. Large fish and birds may be at the top.

The Food Chain

The food chain of a river or lake starts with plant life. You may have seen algae in fish tanks or ponds. It looks green and feels slimy. Algae is a very simple type of plant that produces oxygen. It has no leaves, flowers, or roots. Fish eat algae. Some fish also nibble on other types of plants.

Plants attract insects. They serve as food and as places to lay eggs. Insects and their eggs become food for fish, birds, and amphibians, such as frogs and salamanders.

Of course, big fish eat small fish. Small animals that come to a lake to drink might catch a fish or bird. Or they might become a larger animal's meal.

Breaking the Food Chain

What do you think would happen if there were no plants in a river or lake? Would insects live there? What would birds that feed on insects or fish eat? Would fish thrive? Would fish and birds come around or would they find another place to live?

toxin = any poison-ous substance.
adjective: **toxic**

We've talked about polluted water having poisons, or toxins, in it. When insects and small fish eat or absorb these poisons, larger fish—those higher in the food chain—eat them in turn.

A larger fish that eats fish or insects containing toxins also will be poisoned. The poison might eventually kill it, or the fish might be caught and eaten by another animal higher up the food chain. Clearly, as we go up the food chain, each animal can be poisoned by eating toxic food. An animal need not swim in or drink the polluted water to be poisoned by its toxins.

Large fish can accumulate high levels of toxins in their tissues. They are no longer safe to eat.

Human beings, who might eat fish from a polluted lake, are at the top of the food chain. If you live near a polluted lake, you probably have been warned not to eat fish caught in that lake or at least to limit how much lake fish you eat.

Polluted Lakes

A river's moving water helps it fight the poisons dumped into it. But a river often carries the pollution into a lake. Lake water doesn't move as much as river water does. So the pollution usually stays in the lake for a long time.

44

Lake Tahoe, which lies on the border between California and Nevada, is very deep and very polluted. Because the lake is so deep, it would take more than 700 years for enough water to wash through to carry away all the pollution that is in it now. And since more pollution gets in all the time, the lake has no chance to catch up.

Much of the pollution in lakes comes from nearby farmlands where fertilizers and pesticides have been used. These chemicals are very helpful on farm fields. But when it rains, the runoff water carries these chemicals into nearby lakes.

In small amounts, the nutrients in fertilizers are good for lakes. They help plants to grow. But when a great deal of fertilizer gets into a lake, algae grow too fast. Thick mats of algae cover the surface, preventing sunlight from reaching the other living things in the water.

Lake Tahoe in California (above) is polluted, mostly from farmland runoff. The water collects nutrients from fertilizers, which can cause algae to grow too fast (below).

45

Cleaning It Like a Fish Tank

For more than 50 years, farmers near Delavan Lake in southern Wisconsin used fertilizers containing phosphorus. Year after year, the phosphorus ran off the fields into the lake. By 1980, Delavan Lake had one of the highest phosphorus levels in the nation. Algae grew so thick that fish died. Swimming was almost impossible because a swimmer couldn't see underwater more than three inches (7.5 centimeters)!

The people of Wisconsin started to clean up the lake in 1983.

A sewer system was built around the lake so that the waste from lakeshore houses was no longer dumped into the water. Then, in 1986, a channel was dug along one side of the lake. The river that fed the lake flowed through the new channel to the lake's outlet. The lake was then pumped out until only a few feet of water remained (left).

A chemical called alum was poured into the lake. It combined with the phosphorus, making clumps that fell harmlessly to the bottom. The polluted soil was removed from the bottom. Weeds were pulled out. Then, the lake was allowed to start filling up again. Finally, the engineers created new wetlands along the edges of the lake to collect phosphorus and to filter runoff.

People whose families had lived on Lake Delavan for 100 years or more are pleased with the results. So are the many visitors who enjoy the beautiful water. A swimmer can now see up to 27 feet (8.2 meters) underwater!

Plants need sunlight to change carbon dioxide to oxygen in a process called photosynthesis. When the algae are too thick, other plants don't get enough sunlight. They can't grow, so they don't add new oxygen to the water. Eventually, the fish in the lake die due to lack of oxygen. Gradually, all the living things in the lake die, and the lake itself is regarded as dead. Once this process starts, it's difficult to stop.

The best we can do for most lakes is stop dumping wastes into the water and control the growth of algae. Gradually, nature will clean it up. Some states have laws forbidding the use of laundry detergents that contain chemicals called phosphates. These chemicals also can cause lakes to die.

photosynthesis = the process by which green plants use water, carbon dioxide, and the sun's energy to produce food and oxygen.

The Great Lakes in Trouble

All five of the Great Lakes in the United States and Canada have suffered serious damage from pollution. It's not surprising. Factories, logging and mining companies, and cities on the shores of these lakes have dumped their sewage and wastes into them for almost 300 years.

By the end of the 1970s, Lake Erie was one of the most seriously polluted lakes in the world. Fishermen were forbidden to sell fish caught in its waters. It was called a dead lake.

Finally, in 1986, the eight Midwest states and two Canadian provinces that circle the Great Lakes

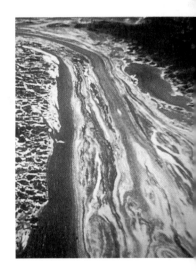

Lake Erie used to be so polluted that it was called a dead lake.

Today, people can use and enjoy the beaches and water of Lake Erie. Salmon also are thriving again in its water.

Scuba divers dove into Lake Erie to remove trash and debris from the bottom of the lake.

got together. They agreed to reduce the dumping of waste into these lakes.

Some factories found new ways to get rid of wastes. Others found new ways to reclaim the water they used to cool their machinery. Some flush all wastes through a cleaning process before they are released. "Pollution police" inspect factories and wastewater plants along the lake shores. Educators teach young people in the area how they can help keep their lakes healthy. However, much more work must be done to get these lakes clean—and keep them that way.

Searching for Solutions

Scientists are trying different solutions to heal damaged lakes all around the world. At Lake

Minnetonka in Minnesota, runoff waters from storms carried a great deal of agricultural fertilizers. Engineers rerouted rain and runoff waters to flow through canals into a nearby wetland before reaching the lake.

These magical cleaners called wetlands are flooded all or part of the year. They also can absorb pollutants. We'll find out more about wetlands in the next chapter.

Officials in Seattle, Washington, decided to dilute the wastes in Green Lake. You can understand dilution if you try a simple experiment: Put some blue food color in half a glass of water. The water turns dark blue. If you add more water, the color becomes lighter. It's been diluted or watered down. In Seattle, they added cleaned and treated wastewater to the lake three times a year. This was not only a good way to reclaim water after treating

The people near Lake Waramaug, Connecticut, cleaned up their lake. As part of the cleanup program, the contaminated soil at the bottom of the lake was removed (left). Today, the water is pumped through a cleaning system before it flows into the lake (right).

Waukegan harbor on Lake Michigan is cleaner today, but sediment at the bottom of the harbor once was so badly polluted with PCBs that it had to be removed.

PCB = a chemical compound produced as a byproduct of industry. PCBs accumulate in animal tissue when released into the environment.

it, but it also helped Green Lake to wash out the wastes trapped in the plants and soil. However, "The Solution to Pollution is Dilution" is no longer thought to be true.

The most expensive way to clean up a lake is to dig up the poisoned bottom soil and replace it with fresh dirt. Some communities have tried this procedure with small lakes and ponds. In Waukegan, Illinois, the bottom of a harbor on Lake Michigan was scooped out. The sediment there was full of toxic chemicals called PCBs from a nearby factory. Today people can eat the fish caught in the harbor. However, removing polluted soil probably is not the answer for many places because it may stir up the pollutants and release them into the water again.

Volunteers for Lakes

The best cure, of course, is prevention—making sure the lakes stay clean in the first place. Many states have organizations like Louisiana's Save Our Lake and Florida's Lake Watch. Volunteers regularly test the water quality in the nearby lakes. They warn people when pollution is getting into the water.

Perhaps you can adopt a lake or pond in your area. Just by picking up the trash on its shores you can help make sure the lake is there for your children, too, to enjoy.

The Save Our Lake organization in Louisiana works to protect and restore Lake Pontchartrain. Volunteers teach children how to protect the lake from pollution (above). They also monitor the lake's water quality to be sure it stays clean (left).

Wetlands, Wonderlands

Lakes are easy to spot as we drive by. But there is another kind of watery place that many people don't notice. They may catch a glimpse of some tall grasses and wildflowers. Or, if they're lucky, they may see a graceful heron or an egret.

Birds are drawn to the special places called wetlands. Like lakes, wetlands can store large amounts of water. In addition, they have a remarkable ability to clean the water that flows through them. These important wetlands also provide the right living conditions for thousands of specially-adapted plants, insects, and other animals.

A wetland is part soil and part water. It's a place where the ground is soggy and full of water

Learning about wetlands will help protect and preserve them. Above, students at a wetland are learning about the animals that live in marshes.

52

at least part of the year. It also takes a special kind of soil to make a wetland, and only certain kinds of plants—those that like to get their "feet" wet—can live in that soil. Cattails are one of the most familiar wetland plants.

Most wetlands lie along another body of water. Most floodplains of rivers are wetlands. Wetlands may lie between the bends in a river, or at the river's mouth. They often can be found along ocean shores mixed with salt water.

See for Yourself

You can see for yourself how some natural wetlands form by creating your own aquifer. You will need a clear glass measuring container; enough aquarium gravel, sand, or clay cat litter to fill the container almost full; a crayon; and some water. First, put gravel, sand, or cat litter in the container. Slowly pour about half a cup of water over the gravel. The water moves through the gravel to the bottom of the bowl. Use the crayon to mark a line at the top of the water. The top of the underground water is called the water table.

Now pour water into the container until you see water in the gravel at the top. The water table has risen. That is what happens to the ground when it rains a lot. But it also happens in a wetland area. Sometimes the water table is near the surface and the ground is wet. At other times, especially during dry summers, the water table

In this wetland, called a sedge meadow, water levels change constantly.

drops much farther. The wetlands may appear to have dried up. When it rains, however, the plant and animal life returns!

Watery Wonderlands

Several different kinds of wetlands are found around the world. These areas can be smaller than a backyard swimming pool or as large as half of a state.

Swamps and marshes are the most familiar wetlands. Swamps sometimes look like watery forests, with trees and other woody plants. Marshes have few trees. They look like a wet field or meadow with grassy and flowering plants.

Wetlands sometimes form all by themselves, with no nearby body of water to feed them. They may develop when a natural depression in the ground fills with water. Soon, some plants start growing in it. They decay into soil, making a better place for other plants to grow. Gradually, a wetland forms.

Bogs are this type of wetland. Their ground is kept spongy from rainfall. A bog may be filled with a moss known as sphagnum. Sphagnum moss also is used by nurseries and flower shops because it can soak up over 100 times its weight of water. You can see how sphagnum bogs might help keep floodwaters under control by acting like a giant sponge. The moss in old bogs sometimes is cut and dried to use as fuel called peat.

Cranberries grow in wetlands called bogs.

The Great Plains of Canada and the United States have many riverless wetlands called prairie potholes. They formed in depressions left when the last Ice Age ended. Many migrating waterbirds stop to rest or feed in the tall grasses of such potholes.

Some wetlands are found along the shores of an ocean or near the mouth of a river where it meets the sea. These are filled with a mixture of fresh water and salt water. The types of plants and fish found in the water depend on how salty it is. The majority of ocean fish species depend on these wetlands for food sources and for breeding grounds where young fish can grow and thrive.

The Nile River of Egypt forms a huge delta at its mouth. This picture was taken from space.

Certain rivers carry much sediment to their mouths. The sediment settles out and often collects in a fan-shaped area called a delta. A delta is another type of wetland.

Wetlands are full of a great variety of life. Plants that live in this soil like having their roots wet. Waterbirds lay their eggs in tall grasses. Crayfish and many other small animals live

in the water. Numerous birds depend on those animals as well as on insects for food. All these creatures are part of a wetland.

An African Delta Survives

The Okavango River in Africa forms the Okavango Delta in Botswana. While most rivers flow either into a lake, another river, or an ocean, this river empties onto the Kalahari Desert. There the river is divided into many small streams that crisscross, creating small islands and lakes in the delta.

The Okavango Delta always has been home to thousands of different species of birds, fish, and mammals. Many of them are threatened or endangered and found only in this one location.

In 1990, the Botswana government decided to drain part of the water from the delta. They wanted to have more water available for diamond mining and several Botswana cities.

But the citizens of the area objected! Along with an international group called Greenpeace, which works to protect the environment, the people protested against the plan. They argued that the survival of the wildlife of the Kalahari Desert, which depends on the delta water, was too important to the world. In March 1991, the government canceled its plans. Another important wetland and its community of plants, animals, and people were saved because people cared and spoke up.

Losing Wetlands

Wetlands are important to our planet. Unfortunately, we didn't realize that until about half the world's wetlands already had been destroyed. Over the centuries, wetlands were drained by digging canals through them. Sometimes they were filled in with soil to create new farmland or sites for waterfront homes.

In the United States, some lost wetland areas are now cities, airports, or harbors. Some wetlands have become farmland, including about half of the Midwest's small wetlands called prairie potholes. Others have been used as garbage dumps. They are so polluted that the living things in them have been killed. Many of our wetlands are gone, along with their wonderful wildlife.

Both for ourselves and for the rest of nature, we must try to preserve or restore our wetlands. The wetlands of the world are among our most important water areas. The kinds of plants that grow in them have a special ability to filter and clean wastewater. And all their plants and grasses attract birds and other wildlife. Many of these birds and animals can't live anywhere else.

Because the population is growing in the San Francisco, California, region, people want to fill in wetlands to build businesses and homes. People are uniting now to save the wetlands for nature.

The Everglades is home to many waterbirds (top). It is also home to the water-loving American alligator (above).

Florida's Everglades

The Everglades is a huge wetland in southern Florida. This unusual wetland is a very shallow river 50 miles (81 kilometers) wide and 100 miles (161 kilometers) long. It contains marsh and swamp areas, tree islands, and pine forests.

Over 400 types of endangered wildlife and plants live here, including the American crocodile. The Florida panther, manatee, wood stork, and Everglades kite have almost disappeared.

The Everglades once covered most of southern Florida. But, like many other wetlands in the United States, large parts of it were drained and turned into farmland. Other parts now are communities and business areas. To make matters worse, the water in this wetland has been polluted severely by fertilizers and other chemical runoff from farms farther north.

The water that supplied the Everglades came from Lake Okeechobee, when it overflowed after rain. But levees were built along the lake's southern shore to keep it from overflowing. The Everglades no longer received enough water. Gradually, life in the Everglades began to die.

Many people in Florida and the rest of the country have tried to stop the destruction of the Everglades. Marjory Stoneman Douglas, who gave the huge wetland its nickname—"River of Grass"—is a leader of the effort. The work is paying off.

At present, the Everglades National Park includes only about 25 percent of its total wetland area. The U.S. government plans to include more of the Everglades in the park. Big Cypress Swamp, which is next to Everglades National Park, is already a wildlife refuge. In this way, the land will be protected and can't be changed. Plans also are being made to open up more waterways to let water reach the wetland.

Marjory Stoneman Douglas led the effort to save the Everglades.

Unfortunately, much of the damage to the Everglades has been done by people far outside the wetland. Unless that damage is stopped, it won't help to make the national park larger. The governor of Florida is raising money to buy back parts of the Everglades from farmers and builders. Some farmers have already promised to turn part of their land into wetlands again. How can they do that? Let's find out.

The Master Marsh Builder

Ed Garbisch, Jr., had a dream. He wanted to help the environ-ment by creating more marshland near the Chesapeake Bay in Maryland. In 1972, he created a company called Environmental Concern. Hambleton Island was being washed away by the natural

churning of the ocean waves on the bay. Garbisch and some of his friends hoped they could stop the island's soil from eroding by rebuilding a marsh on the edge of the island.

First, they filled in the edge of the island with sand so that marsh grasses could grow. The roots of these marsh grasses hold the sand and soil in place and keep them from being washed away. It took five months to plant the grass seedlings and for the roots to take hold. The new plant life helped protect the filled-in area from being washed away again. Some sea animals, insects, and fish discovered the area and made the rebuilt marsh their new home. Other fish and plants were brought from nearby wetlands.

Today, Ed Garbisch's company restores or creates dozens of saltwater marshes each year on the East Coast of the United States. Along with marsh builders throughout the world, he is making our planet a better and healthier place to live.

How to Build an Artificial Wetland

Some farmers in Florida will replace wetlands near the Everglades. That sounds very strange—surely only nature can make a wetland.

An artificial wetland may be just big enough to handle the wastewater from your bathtub. Or it can be large enough to clean up all the wastewater from a large city.

Before wetland builders start their work, they carefully study the area to be served by the wetland. Most new wetlands are created around a series of two or more pools. Each pool, or cell, is designed to do a specific job.

The bottom of the new wetland area is lined with gravel of various sizes. Plants are brought in and planted in the gravel. Cattails especially are good for the first pool of a freshwater wetland where the pollution might be strongest. A grass called cordgrass is useful where ocean tides bring saltwater into the wetland.

Wetlands built to keep areas from eroding or washing away need bushes and grasses with deep roots. Wetlands built to treat wastewater need plants that gobble up the nutrients in fertilizer and sewage.

Snails, worms, tiny floating animals, and special kinds of fish also are added to wastewater marshes to help eat bacteria. Striped bass have been added to some wastewater marshes that have

Artificial wetlands are lined with gravel (top). Plants such as cattails are then planted (middle). Sometimes striped bass (bottom) are added to marshes.

AN ARTIFICIAL WETLAND

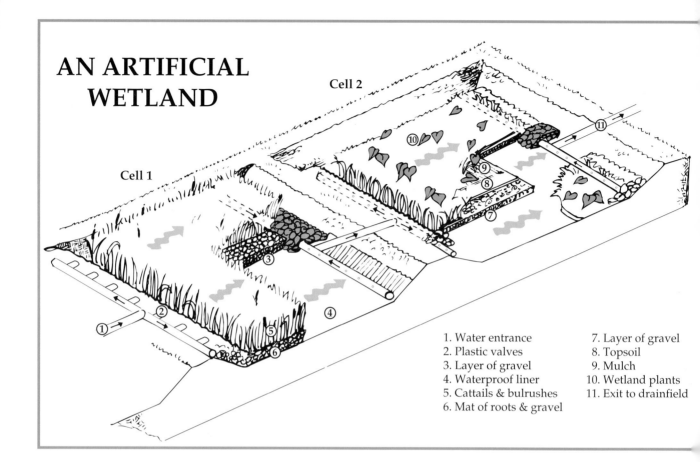

Cell 1

Cell 2

1. Water entrance
2. Plastic valves
3. Layer of gravel
4. Waterproof liner
5. Cattails & bulrushes
6. Mat of roots & gravel
7. Layer of gravel
8. Topsoil
9. Mulch
10. Wetland plants
11. Exit to drainfield

An artifical wetland consists of more than one pool, or cell. Water is cleaned by wetland plants and animals as it flows through the different pools.

more than one pool. Usually the bass are found in the second or third pool where the water is cleaner. These bass can be used later to stock local lakes.

Frogs, insects, and other wetland animals are brought in from other local marshes. They enjoy their new wetland home and build up the animal community of the new marsh.

Finally, the experts plant bushes and trees around the wetland. The area starts to look like a woodland or park. It might attract wildlife and provide them with food and shelter.

Each year, wetland scientists learn more and

A Wetland for Wildlife

One of the earliest and most famous artificial wetland projects is in Arcata, California. In the 1970s, the people there had a problem many cities face. Their wastewater-treatment plant wasn't able to process all the wastewater the town created.

Instead of building more wastewater-treatment plants, Arcata was among the first cities to build an artificial wetland. Wastewater first goes through filters and some preparatory treatments. Then it travels through a series of artificial marshes. In the marshes, a combination of plants and fish break down bacteria and waste products and help purify the water. After about two months, the water is returned to the treatment center. Specialists add chemicals to the water to kill any remaining bacteria. When the water is piped to a bay in the Pacific Ocean, it is actually cleaner than water from wastewater-treatment plants.

Arcata also has made the area around the wetlands a good place for wildlife. More than 200 species of birds enjoy life there.

more about wetlands, how they work, and how they can be constructed. Artificial wetlands are becoming an important tool in restoring the Earth.

"Living Machine" Waste Treatment

When you walk through Dr. John Todd's greenhouse at the Center for the Restoration of Water at Ocean Arks International in Maryland, you don't see roses or houseplants. Instead, large tanks of water are filled with growing things. They look a little like small wetlands. Dr. Todd calls this a "Living Machine."

Wastewater flows from tank to tank in Dr. John Todd's "Living Machine."

Raw wastewater enters the greenhouse. It flows from tank to tank, getting cleaner and cleaner as it moves among the gravel and plant roots. By the time it reaches the last tank, the water is crystal clear. The sun makes this machine run.

The secret to Todd's success is knowing what plants to put in each tank. Various plants and life-forms absorb different nutrients from the waste stream. It took him several years to discover the right order and combinations.

Cities and towns that have tried Todd's technique are very happy with the results. Since the "Living Machine" takes up less room than a typical wastewater treatment plant or artificial wetland, he may have found the key to the future of wastewater treatment.

The Future of Wetlands

In the past, we destroyed wetlands. In the future, we'll be building more. But we can't depend on artificial wetlands alone. We must take care of the natural wetlands we still have.

Billions of people live on our planet, and the population increases each year. We all need food to eat, water to drink, and somewhere to live. Farmers need more land to grow more crops, and the soil in wetlands is filled with nutrients, which makes it excellent.

People need land to build communities, and wetlands are all too easy to fill in. Somehow we need to find a balance between our requirements and nature's needs.

In 1975, many countries signed an agreement called the Ramsar Convention. Each country promised to protect at least one major wetland within its borders. By June 1993, 610 wetland sites had been listed for protection, including the one below at Delaware Bay.

Oceans and Harbors

Just past midnight on March 24, 1989, an oil tanker called the *Exxon Valdez* struck a reef in Prince William Sound, Alaska. More than 11 million gallons (42 million liters) of oil spilled out into the sea. Thick black oil spread over 1,200 miles (1,935 kilometers) of shoreline.

On the first day alone, thousands of birds, sea otters, and other marine animals died. The numbers grew worse with each passing day. We'll never know exactly how many sea mammals, fish, and birds sank to the ocean floor. That one accident may well have changed life in Alaskan waters permanently.

When the Exxon Valdez *ran aground on Bligh Reef in Prince William Sound, Alaska, millions of gallons of oil spilled into the water (above).*

An Oily Mess

Oil seeps into ocean waters every day, from both human facilities and natural cracks in the seafloor. The water in harbors always has a rainbow film of oil on the surface. Boat engines use oil to keep running smoothly and some seems always to get into the water.

Oil companies often drill in the ocean floor to reach oil under the sea. They drill from special platforms anchored out in the open sea. Large underwater pipes or seagoing tankers carry the oil to storage tanks on land. These may leak and allow oil to spill into the ocean.

It seems as if every time oil is handled—from when it is found underground to when it is taken from the refinery to a gas station or factory—some of it spills. Those spills are harming the largest bodies of water on Earth—the oceans.

But not all the oil that gets into oceans comes from spills. All over the world there are places where oil from deep underground rises to the surface. The Santa Barbara Channel off California is one such natural oil seep.

Oil seeps into the water in many different ways. It forms a colorful but dangerous film on top of the water.

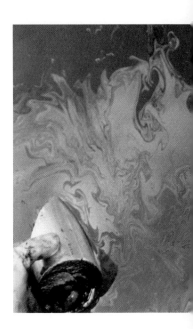

Long–Term Effects

It costs billions of dollars to repair the damage caused by oil spills. The Exxon company spent $2.5 billion to clean up the Alaskan spill. But no amount of money could bring the mammals and

Thousands of birds are killed when oil spills into waterways

birds back to life. Nor could it repair the damage done to the food chain in that part of the ocean.

Thousands of animals starved to death because their normal foods no longer were available. And when they ate oil-coated seaweed or licked oil off their fur, the animals died. The oil spill harmed herring reproduction, permanently polluted shell-fish beds, and continues to poison sea otters and harbor seals. It killed hundreds of thousands of birds.

Shellfish and salmon in those waters also absorbed the toxins. Native fishermen couldn't eat or sell their catches. Many people who depended on fishing had to move to other areas.

Of the money that the Exxon company paid to clean up the oil spill, $1.2 billion will go to the U.S. government over a period of ten years. This money will be used to find ways to restore Prince William Sound.

Cleanup Efforts

Many new ideas for cleaning oil spills have been suggested in recent years. Some cost too much to use on huge spills. Others cause almost as much damage as the oil.

Strong detergents, which are chemical compounds, have been sprayed on oil spills. They break up the oil quickly, but they do not remove it from the water. Also, detergents can be as dangerous as oil to fish and marine life.

Powdered chalk soaks up oil until the increasing weight causes it to sink. But that leaves oil on the seafloor where it still can damage living things. And it remains in the sand for generations.

Products like straw and Styrofoam are sometimes spread out over the oil to absorb it, and then are scooped up. The problem with this method is that it works only in small areas and where the water is calm. Also, the oil-soaked material then must be disposed of, which can prove to be an even larger problem.

Since oil floats on top of water, large floating barriers called booms can be placed around a spill to keep the oil from spreading. Booms work very well if they are put in place soon enough. Pumps then suck up the oil from the surface. Again, this idea works only with small spills and calm waters.

The truth is that we have no good answers for cleaning up oil spills. Maybe you'll invent a solution to this enormous problem.

When the water is calm and oil spills are small, booms can stop oil from spreading.

Scientists are experimenting with a new way to clean up oil spills. They spray special bacteria onto the oil. These microscopic creatures digest the oil.

69

Unfortunately, every country depends on oil for energy. So, for now, the most—and least—we can do is prevent oil from spilling into the ocean in the first place.

A Watery Trash Can

Twenty billion tons of waste are dumped into our oceans near coastal areas every year. It's hard to imagine that much garbage. Some of it has been treated in wastewater-treatment plants. Some of it is raw waste, full of dangerous bacteria and toxins.

Ocean currents carry trash that is dumped in one spot to pollute water and beaches in another. For years, New York and other East Coast cities took their trash out to sea on ships. At a certain spot, the ships dumped their loads.

Then, in 1987, tons of discarded wastes washed up on the shores of New Jersey. People walking along the beaches found decaying garbage, dead fish and dolphins, tubes of blood, and even soiled needles and bandages. The beaches were closed until the garbage could be cleaned up.

Much of the waste thrown into the sea is biodegradable. The movement of the sea breaks it down and its nutrients are reused by marine life. But some garbage and most of the waste that comes from factories cannot be broken down naturally. And such water carries oils and chemicals that are toxic to life in the ocean.

A Death Trap Called Plastic

They seem so innocent—the plastic rings that hold a six-pack of soda cans together, or the plastic bag your sandwich came in. You can walk along some beaches and find enough plastic to fill a garbage can in a few minutes.

Our beaches are not the only victims of the "plastic war." Fish, seabirds, turtles, sea otters, dolphins, porpoises, whales, and penguins often mistake plastic for a piece of food, such as a jelly-fish. It gets stuck in the animal's throat or fills its stomach so that it soon starves.

In 1988, a Texas scientist examined 110 dead sea turtles he found on the shores along the Gulf of Mexico. He found that 63 of them had plastic in their stomachs. That year, an international law was passed to stop the dumping of plastic trash in the ocean.

Between six and seven billion pounds (2.7 and 3.1 billion kilograms) of trash are disposed of at sea every year. Over half of the waste that washes up on beaches is plastic.

The six-pack rings can get caught around the throats of young animals. As they grow, the rings slowly choke them. The state of Maine has outlawed the sale of six-packs held together with plastic rings.

You can make sure that no animal gets caught in the rings of one of your six-packs by cutting each ring before you throw the plastic in your recycling bin.

Red Tides

We know that when fertilizers get into the water of a lake, algae may grow too thick. Something similar happens in oceans.

In oceans, the extra algae has room to grow. Eventually it dies and sometimes the dead plant matter turns toxic. Marine animals that swim through it or eat it get sick. A bed of toxic algae is known as a red tide, because the first ones observed were red. But algae blooms also can be green, brown, or yellow, depending on the type of algae.

Red tides have occurred for many years, and they are not always caused by pollution. Red tides also occur naturally. Sometimes we don't understand why there is a sudden explosion of algae. But we know we must keep our oceans as clean as possible to cut down on red tides.

red tide = a large mass of toxic, decaying algae in the sea, often caused by pollution.

In 1987, off the coast of the Carolinas, a red tide killed almost the entire population of sea scallops.

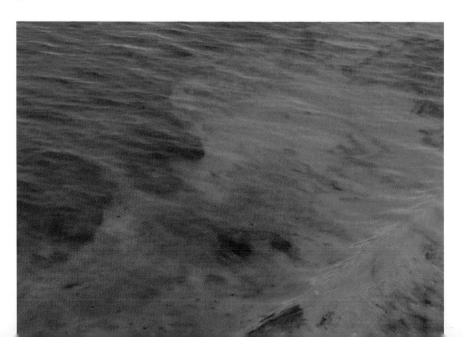

Living Things Suffer

One group of white beluga whales lives in North America's St. Lawrence River. When one of these gentle creatures dies, its body is handled like toxic waste. Why? For decades, these whales have eaten fish from the river. Toxic pollution made the fish too dangerous for people to eat—but no one told the whales.

Off Imperial Beach, just north of California's Baja region, surfers have been getting sick after spending the day in the water. They develop rashes and sores on their skin and flulike symptoms. Studies show high amounts of bacteria in that part of the Pacific Ocean.

The source of the bacteria seems to be the Tijuana River in Mexico, which empties into the Pacific near Imperial Beach. Factories and cities along the river are dumping large amounts of contaminated wastes containing disease-causing bacteria directly into the water.

Keeping pollution out of the oceans is the only way to protect them and the living things in them. To help solve the problem at Imperial Beach, the United States government has asked Mexico to let Americans build a wastewater-treatment plant along the river. Then the waste that is causing the problem might never reach the ocean. What doesn't go into the water can't hurt the wildlife or the environment.

The population of beluga whales in the St. Lawrence River is shrinking because the water is polluted. Canada is trying to stop pollution and save the whales.

Rain on City Streets

Most of the pollution that goes into the ocean does not come from factories or wastewater plants. Under your city there are two sets of pipes. The pipes that go into your house go to and from wastewater-treatment plants.

The other pipes are called storm drains. They carry away water that washes off the streets and parking lots after rain.

But water that flows through storm drains carries more than just rain. It also carries urban runoff—all the dirt, oil, rotting food, and other trash thrown on our streets. This filthy water can be harmful to our water supplies.

In many cities, the water that goes through storm drains never goes into wastewater-treatment centers. It flows directly into the ocean. Inland cities usually send the water into rivers or lakes. That water also can reach the sea eventually.

Cities and towns sweep streets on a regular basis. This keeps trash and other debris out of storm drains.

Heal the Bay

Santa Monica Bay near Los Angeles, California, has a group of dedicated people watching out for its good health. The organization—called Heal the Bay group—has a Gutter Patrol Program. Many volunteers spend weekends sweeping streets and making sure that storm drains are clean. They also help teach people why it's bad for the environment to throw trash into storm drains.

Every year an organization called Heal the Bay organizes a special beach cleanup called Coastal Cleanup Day (left). Heal the Bay volunteers also stencil storm drains with a message reminding people that the water from storm drains empties into the ocean (below).

Once a year, on Coastal Cleanup Day, Heal the Bay organizes many people to clean up the beach. These helpful people have made a big difference. Several years ago, Santa Monica Bay was suffering the effects of heavy pollution. Today, sea life is starting to return to normal. Shellfish, fish, and plants live in the waters, and the ocean is safe for swimming once again.

Unsalting the Sea

It's important to keep the sea clean for the benefit of the creatures that live in it. But it's also important for us. Someday we all might need the sea for our drinking water. Even now, some places remove the salt from seawater in a process called desalination so that it's safe to drink.

desalination = the process of removing salt from seawater.

75

We Don't Dump Trash into Your House

One morning in 1984, a group of southern California surfers decided to do something about the disgusting condition of the ocean. They were tired of swimming in trash, soda cans, plastic bags, and sewage. These ocean lovers formed the Surfrider Foundation.

The Surfrider Foundation is a national organization. It helps the government find companies that damage our oceans and break water-pollution laws. A few years ago, the Surfriders made sure two paper mills in northern California stopped dumping wastes in the ocean. Before they could continue operating, these companies had to pay over $10 million in damages and spend over $110 million making changes in their factories.

The Surfriders' Blue Water Task Force helps keep track of the ocean's condition. Area residents take test kits to the beach, collect samples of the water, and call in the results. A laboratory lets Surfriders know if the bacteria count in the water has increased. Classrooms of local students often use the kits for science projects. Surfriders also stencil signs like the one shown here on storm drains.

Education is an important part of their program. Surfrider Brad Gerlach sums it up: "If I lived among the trees, I'd protect the trees. But I live in the water. I spend most of my waking moments there. We're kind of like dolphins that came to land to explain what it's really like to live in the water, like fish. But fish can't come up and say, 'Hey, guys, what's up?' "

Santa Catalina Island, off the coast of southern California, has a desalination plant. It provides about 25 percent of the island's fresh water.

The simplest way to remove the salt from water is to let the sun evaporate the water. The salt stays behind. The water vapor can be turned back into liquid and collected. People have desalted water by evaporation since ancient times.

Today, machines use a combination of heat and filters to separate salt from seawater. Other machines work by freezing the water. However, most machines to desalt water can handle only small amounts of water at a time. They are too small for most cities to use.

The Middle Eastern nation of Saudi Arabia gets much of its fresh water from huge desalination plants on the Persian Gulf. However, Saudi Arabia sells oil all over the world, so it can afford to desalinate sea water.

Turning sea water into fresh water is a very expensive process. It can cost five to ten times more than pumping water from lakes or aquifers. Also, it takes more energy to desalinate water than to pump it from underground. Scientists are working hard to make desalination more affordable in the future.

Our Oceans Today

Do the toxic white beluga whales show what might happen to people? Huge quantities of fish

and other seafood help feed the world's people. Oceans are a major source of oxygen for the atmosphere. We also depend on our oceans for food and for products we use almost every day. Some of these products surprise us. For example, did you know that ice cream is made with small amounts of kelp, a kind of algae?

Ice cream is made with small amounts of an ocean-growing algae called giant kelp (left).

Our oceans and shores are affected by oil spills, red tides, polluted harbors, and storm drain runoff. Making sure our oceans stay clean and healthy is the responsibility of every nation and all the people of the world.

Our oceans and beaches need to be protected from all types of pollution.

Groundwater, Buried Treasure

Wells are drilled to reach the underground water supply (above). Individuals and cities use this water for a variety of needs.

We may not live near a freshwater river or lake, but we still need fresh water. We need it daily for drinking, cooking, washing, and watering crops.

For thousands of years, people have known they could get water from the ground. They would dig a deep hole and hope that water would bubble out. But sometimes they had to dig many holes before they reached underground water supplies.

If you live in the country, you might have a well in your backyard. That well reaches down into an aquifer. Most wells have pumps that draw the water from the ground. However, the water in artesian wells is confined. The pressure forces the water to rise to the surface by itself.

Groundwater aquifers hold 30 times more water than all the world's freshwater lakes. They also hold more than 3,000 times the amount of water in our streams and rivers.

Usually groundwater is very clean. The rocks, soil, and gravel above the aquifer filter out much of the waste in the water. If you live in a city, groundwater also goes through a wastewater-treatment plant.

The Ogallala Aquifer

The largest aquifer in the United States lies under the states of Texas, Oklahoma, New Mexico, Kansas, Colorado, Nebraska, Wyoming, and South Dakota. Farmers discovered this aquifer in the late 1800s. Families in South Dakota said the water shot 100 feet (30 meters) in the air when the first wells were dug. Finding the aquifer meant that a huge section of the country without much surface water could be opened for settlement and cattle grazing.

But the Ogallala Aquifer is not limitless. Its water level has dropped one to five feet (0.3 to 1.5 meters) every year. As more wells were dug in the area, the pressure in all the wells dropped. Wells then had to be deeper and more electricity was required to pump the water to the surface. Today, this aquifer provides water for over 170,000 wells.

When the Ogallala Aquifer was discovered, thousands of acres of land in the Great Plains had water for farming.

So much water was pumped from the ground beneath this well in Arizona that the land sank, breaking the concrete.

That Sinking Feeling

In Mexico City, a large cathedral tilts downward on the right side. In Tokyo, Japan, the ground under houses and buildings in the eastern part of the city is slowly sinking. And in Bangkok, Thailand, the land sinks five inches (13 centimeters) each year.

Is someone digging under the cities of the world? No, but something valuable is being removed from underneath these areas—water.

If you pump water out of a lake faster than a river can refill it, the level of water in the lake goes down. That's happening in many aquifers today. The water that takes up space and supports the land is being used faster than it is being replaced.

Farmers Saving Water

Obviously, the best way to keep aquifers full is to use less water. Growing crops require a lot of water. Farmers use almost 75 percent of all the fresh water pumped each year in California.

The Central Valley of California, where many crops are grown, gets very hot in the summer. A great deal of water evaporates from irrigation ditches before it even reaches the plants. Also, water soaks into the ground before it can be used.

The city of Los Angeles built new ditches for some farmers. They lined the ditches with concrete so that water couldn't leak into the ground. The farmers saved so much water they had extra to sell to the city.

When ditches are lined with concrete, water is conserved because it cannot soak into the ground.

In 1993 the city of Phoenix, Arizona, also made a deal with nearby farmers. For every two gallons (7.5 liters) of fresh water the farmers pump from wells and give to the city, they get three gallons (11 liters) of treated wastewater to use on crops. It's a good deal for everyone. The farmers have more water, the city gets much-needed drinking water, and the environment is helped in the process.

Helping Nature Fill the Aquifers

The city of El Paso, Texas, is doing something to refill its aquifer. It pumps treated wastewater back into the ground. The water takes two to four years to filter through the soil and the rocks until it becomes available in the aquifer again. But that water would not have been available if it hadn't

A Spoonful of Water?

Israel's scientists developed a new system for irrigating crops in a hot, dry country where water evaporates quickly. Most farmers around the world irrigate by spraying water in the air over their crops. But the Israeli farmers have buried pipes in the ground. Water drips from holes in the pipes right onto the roots of the growing plants.

This "drip irrigation" technique has cut Israel's use of water by more than 30 percent! The crops also seem to benefit. Plants are producing more fruits and vegetables.

The Israeli technique is so successful that many farms in other dry areas of the world are burying water pipes. Not only is it water efficient, but using this technique will enable farmers to feed many more people.

Some Israeli farms use computers to save water. Measuring devices placed in the ground near the crops "read" how much water is in the soil. The computers decide when and how much to water the crops. This keeps the farmers from over watering and thus wasting water.

been pumped down into the ground. Unfortunately, water replacement is very expensive.

Other cities have built artificial wetlands and lakes. Some of the water slowly soaks into the ground and enters an aquifer as it usually does during the water cycle. This process is less expensive than pumping the water into the ground, but the water is not available for several years.

Gas tanks that have been buried in the ground can develop unseen leaks. The groundwater can be polluted before the leaks are found. The federal government controls underground tanks very carefully.

Pollutants into the Ground

The water in aquifers usually stays fairly clean, but more and more toxic petroleum is seeping into the ground and the aquifers due to oil spills. Sometimes underground gasoline tanks leak. No one is aware of the leak until the water in nearby wells begins to taste bad. And such spills are almost impossible to clean up completely.

On Long Island, New York, an underground gasoline tank leaked for a long time without anyone knowing. Then the gasoline company discovered their gasoline floating on top of the aquifer!

They dug a series of wells and pumped off the liquid gasoline. Then they began to pump water out of the aquifer and treated the water to clean it. The cleaned water was pumped into special ponds. From the ponds, it settled back into the aquifer. This was a long, slow, and expensive process, but it was the only way to be sure that the people of Long Island had good drinking water.

Another source of groundwater pollution is garbage dumps. For many years, cities have dumped their solid waste in pits. When one pit filled up, we just dug another. We thought all the garbage would break down eventually and become dirt. We were wrong. Most of the garbage stays the same for many years.

We've also learned that each time it rains, some of the water runs through the trash. As it soaks through the garbage, it picks up toxins and other chemicals from the trash. The polluted water then

Homeowners in Setauket, Long Island, watch as a well is drilled in their front yard after an underground gas tank leak was discovered.

The Air Force Cleans Up

McClellan Air Force Base in California had an unusual problem. This base does aircraft repairs. Over the years, the ground in the repair areas had soaked up toxic oil and paint. Each time the ground got wet, the water carried more and more toxic chemicals into the aquifer.

The Air Force decided it was time to get serious about cleaning up the aquifer. They dug some wells and started to pump up the polluted water. They put it through a treatment plant (above) to remove the unwanted chemicals. The treated water is used to cool machinery on the base and to water lawns. It also is piped into a nearby wetland area where it is cleaned even further.

Of course, the Air Force realized that it would have been easier to keep the groundwater clean in the first place. They now are working hard to do just that.

runs into rivers and streams or soaks down into our groundwater.

To correct this problem, special places called sanitary landfills now are used for solid waste. They are lined with plastic so that water can't soak through them into the groundwater. Every day, after garbage is dumped, a layer of soil is spread across the top. Gradually the landfill becomes a hill. Set into the hill are special wells where the runoff liquid accumulates. It is pumped out and disposed of in places where it can't hurt our water. Some landfills have computers to keep track of what's happening inside them. It is now against the law to throw any toxic or dangerous items into a landfill.

A sanitary landfill has a heavy plastic liner on the bottom to keep polluted water from soaking into the ground.

Making Landfill Runoff Helpful

Even the best-designed landfill has water that runs from inside the hill. The state of New York may have a solution. It collects all the water that runs through landfills and directs it into an artificial wetland. In the wetland, special plants absorb many harmful toxins before the water seeps down into the groundwater.

Building more wastewater-treatment plants can be very expensive. By letting nature do the work, New York not only saved money but also created new wetland areas for people and wildlife to enjoy.

Giving Mother Nature a Hand

When the people of Clayton County, Georgia, realized that their local rivers just couldn't accept any more treated wastewater, they decided to imitate nature. In the process, they improved the environment, made a forest productive, and helped the water cycle refill their aquifer.

Today, their treated wastewater isn't dumped. It's sprayed over a forest. About 2.5 inches (7 centimeters) of man-made rain falls every day on the forest, enough to make it almost a tropical rain forest. The water that isn't absorbed by the leaves and roots makes its way down into the aquifer and becomes groundwater.

The trees absorb some of the extra nutrients in the wastewater and grow very quickly. Part of the forest is cut down every year and new trees are planted. The harvested trees are ground up as wood chips. Some of the chips are burned to run factory machines. The rest get mixed in with the processed sludge from the wastewater treatment. It is used to help fertilize forests and other county property.

This industrial plant in Kentucky uses an artificial wetland to clean its wastewater.

In developing countries such as Colombia in South America, a new water pipe will deliver cleaner water to the people.

Improving the Blue Planet

We've discussed many new ideas on how to improve the quality and quantity of water on our planet. Scientists and engineers always are finding ways to improve the way we handle water, both before and after we use it. Wastewater-treatment plants are more efficient than ever before. Every improvement brings us closer to the day we'll drink reclaimed water. Maybe someday we'll say that reclaimed water tastes better than our "old" water. It will definitely be cleaner than the water we drink today. Then we truly will have made water into a resource we can use over and over.

Earth has been called the "Blue Planet" and the "Water Planet." It can remain so only if people help. We must save all the water we can. We must keep pollutants of all kinds out of our waters. We must restore the water we have damaged in the past—and find new ways to do it.

Let's make sure that our planet's water is safe to drink and plentiful. It's up to us.

We need to make sure we have enough clean water for the people of future generations.

PLACES TO WRITE

You can get more information or find out what you can do to help by writing to one of these organizations:

American River Conservation Council
801 Pennsylvania Ave., SE
Washington, DC 20003

Clean Water Action
1320 18th St., NW
Washington, DC 20036

Coast Alliance
235 Pennsylvania Ave., SE
Washington, DC 20003

Environmental Concern
P.O. Box P
St. Michaels, MD 21663

Friends of the Crooked River
2390 Kensington Road
Akron, OH 44333

Greenpeace USA
1436 U St., NW
Washington, DC 20009

National Wildlife Federation
1412 16th St., NW
Washington, DC 20036

Surfrider Foundation
122 S. El Camino Real
San Clemente, CA 92672

UN Environmental Program
2 UN Plaza
New York, NY 10022

US Environmental Protection Agency
401 M St., SW
Washington, DC 20460

US Fish and Wildlife Service
Dept. of Interior
Washington, DC 20240

US Forest Service
P.O. Box 96090
Washington, DC 20090

US Geological Survey
National Center
Reston, VA 22092

GLOSSARY

algae – single-celled or many-celled plants which contain chlorophyll

aquifer – an underground rock formation where water is stored and through which it can move. It has a bottom of solid rock.

bacteria – one-celled living things that may cause disease; so small that they can be seen only with a microscope.

biodegradable – able to be broken down into natural chemicals and then reused by nature.

desalination – the process of removing salt from sea water.

evaporate – change from a liquid into a gas.

fertilizers – animal waste or chemicals that add nutrients to soil to help crops grow.

floodplain – the land across which a river normally floods.

groundwater – fresh water that moves through and among the rocks underground.

levee – a barrier made of packed soil and rock built alongside a river to keep it from flooding over the land.

nutrients – substances needed by plants and animals to grow and live.

parasite – any living thing that grows, feeds, and is sheltered at the expense of another.

PCB - a chemical compound produced as a by-product of industry. PCBs accumulate in animal tissue when released into the environment.

pesticides - chemicals that kill insects, weeds, and other pests on crops.

photosynthesis - process by which green plants use water, carbon dioxide, and the sun's energy to produce food and oxygen.

pollution – harmful chemicals or other materials that don't belong in the environment.

reclaimed water – wastewater that is partially cleaned and treated. It is used to water crops and lawns, but not to drink.

recycle – to reuse water and other materials instead of throwing them away.

red tide – a large mass of toxic, decaying algae in the sea, often caused by pollution.

runoff – water that runs over the surface of the ground before reaching a lake, a river, or the ocean.

sediment – debris such as bits of leaves, dead animals, loose soil, and clay that settles out of water and onto the bottom of a waterway.

sludge – the almost solid material that settles out when used water is cleaned in a wastewater-treatment plant.

species – one kind of animal or plant. Members of a species usually can breed only with each other.

toxin – any poisonous substance. adjective: **toxic**

tributary – a stream or smaller river that flows into a larger river.

wastewater – water that has been used in some way and is no longer clean; also called sewage.

wetland – land that has water standing in it all or part of the year.

INDEX

Gulf of Mexico 71
Gutter Patrol Program 74

H

Hambleton Island, Maryland 60
harbor seals 68
harbors 50, 66-67, 79
Heal the Bay 74
Hindu people 38
Hoover Dam 7
hydrologic cycle 19

I

Ice Age 55
ice cap 8
ice cream 79
Illinois 50
Imperial Beach 73
India 14, 38-39
Industrial Age 9
insects 12, 43-44, 52, 62
irrigation 29, *see* drip irrigation
irrigation ditches 83
Irvine, California 26
Israel 84

J

Japan 82
jellyfish 71

K

Kalahari Desert 56
Kansas 81
kelp 79
Kentucky 90
Kerr-McGee 70
Kissimmee River 33

L

Lake Erie 47-48
Lake Michigan 23, 50
Lake Okeechobee 34, 59
Lake Pontchartrain 51
Lake Superior 42
Lake Tahoe 45
Lake Waramaug 49
Lake Watch 51
lakes 6-7, 8, 9, 13, 20-25, 42-45, 47-
  48, 51, 72, 78, 80-82
landfills 24

leaking underground storage tanks
  85-86
levees 11, 20, 30, 32, 33, 59
logging 47
Long Island 86
Los Angeles, California 74
Louisiana 11, 32, 51

M

Maine 71
mammals 56
manatee 58
manufacturing 22, 38, *see* factories
manure 12
marsh 8, 11, 52, 54, 60-63
Maryland 60, 64
Massachusetts 35
McClellan Air Force Base 87
Mexico 73, 82
Mexico City 82
Miami, Florida 9
Midwest 30, 57
Milorganite 23
mining 47, 56
Mississippi River 11, 30-31
Missouri 30-31
Missouri River 83

N

Nebraska 81
Nevada 45
New Jersey 70
New Mexico 81
New Orleans, Louisiana 32
New York 86, 88
Nile River 55
North America 14, 24, 42, 73
North Sea 40
nutrients 10, 36, 45, 61, 64-65, 70

O

Ocean Arks International 64
oceans 6-9, 10, 13, 20, 23, 25, 40, 66-
  67, 71-76, 78-79
Ogallala Aquifer 81
Ohio 4, 6, 13, 37-38
oil 40, 66-70, 78. 87
oil spills 68, 79, 85
oil tanker 66
Okavango Delta 56

Oklahoma 81
Ontario 25
organizations 92
oxygen 43, 47, 79

P

Pacific Ocean 63, 73
parasite 22
PCBs 50
peat 54
Persian Gulf 78
pesticides 13, 35, 45
Phoenix, Arizona 83
phosphorus 46
photosynthesis 47
plants 7, 13, 20, 43, 45, 47, 52-53, 60,
  63, 84
plastic 71, 76, 88
plumbing 18, 25
poisons 13, 40, 44
pollutants 10, 40, 49-50
pollution 6, 10, 12, 13, 39, 44-48, 50,
  51, 72-76, 79, 86
ponds 42, 86
population 9
porpoises 71
prairie potholes 55, 57
Prince William Sound, Alaska 66, 68

Q

Quashnet River 35

R

rain 20, 30-31, 36, 45, 53-54, 74, 86,
  89
Ramsar Convention 65
reclaimed water 26, 29, 48-49, 90
  see gray water
recycling 71
Red River 11
red tides 72, 79
renewable resource 90
Rio Quijos 15
river dolphin 39
River of Grass 59
riverbanks 10
RiverDay 4, 6
rivers 4-7, 8, 9-10, 13, 20, 22-23, 25,
  30, 32, 36, 38, 43-44, 55, 80-81,
  88-89

ABOUT THE AUTHOR

Linda Goldman has been writing books and newspaper and magazine articles for children for over 14 years. She loves writing nonfiction because her job is never boring. She's been slimed by an elephant, kissed by a pelican, gone up in a blimp, talked with NASA officials, and met many interesting people. She lives in San Diego, California, with her husband, two cats, and a parakeet. She loves visiting classrooms and talking with students about writing.

The author wishes to thank all the companies and agencies who provided information for this book. A special thanks to Kris Flaig, Associate Process Engineer, Dept. of Public Works, Los Angeles, California. for his technical advice and to my husband, Jay Foley, for his inspiration, ideas, and moral support.